LINES FROM THE EXILE

LINES FROM THE EXILE

Poems for the Outcast, the Reject, and the Refugee

Gregory Hartley

RESOURCE *Publications* · Eugene, Oregon

LINES FROM THE EXILE
Poems for the Outcast, the Reject, and the Refugee

Resource Publications
An Imprint of Wipf and Stock Publishers
199 W. 8th Ave., Suite 3
Eugene, OR 97401

www.wipfandstock.com

PAPERBACK ISBN: 978-1-6667-3843-8
HARDCOVER ISBN: 978-1-6667-9914-9
EBOOK ISBN: 978-1-6667-9915-6

APRIL 4, 2022 11:28 AM

Contents

3. SCHISM

4. REFUGEE

8. Relegatio

9. Intestate

Preface

ONE DAY IN THE spring of 2017, without warning, I lost my job. I had worked with this organization my entire adult life. Twenty years of commitment vanished during a cold, "nothing personal" meeting. My kids, my wife, and I had all spent most of our lives in Florida. Suddenly, we had to leave.

People get fired all the time; this we knew. And employers wield stunning power over their employees. But those issues had always been someone else's problem. Now that problem came to roost, and our lives got canceled in an instant.

With only four months to land a new job, my desperate search spanned the entire country. After 175 applications, only a single, unexpected offer came: from Alaska, of all places. With the overwhelming feeling that we had been evicted and sent into exile, we sold off most of our household and drove the 5,000 miles from Orlando to Anchorage, arriving disoriented and numb.

The great beauty of the state only partially tempered our loss. The move caused an existential crisis: It was like experiencing death while somehow still living. Who were we without our friends and possessions? The losses were not merely material. Our mental stability toppled. A kind of amnesia set in. No longer did we expect life to go our way or the future to be secure. Ultimately, we lost faith. At least for a while.

In order to cope, I began writing, inspired, in part, by Alaska's marching stone spires topped with alpine meadows and blue glaciers. This book is the result of that minor exodus and the prolonged sadness that followed the shockwave of being rejected by our homeland.

As I wrote these poems, the theme of Exile made itself known. So many millions have experienced worse or had lost even more. We could now relate to those social dilemmas that had before remained muted by our comfort and plenty. Those other refugees had not only been cast off but tormented for their beliefs or just their skin color. We became aware of a global surge of alienation caused by racism, sexism, climate change, social media, or religious persecution. Those voices became louder, pressing forward, clamoring for a voice. The work gradually became less about my experience and more about theirs.

I now realize that Exile is not my problem. It is my answer. Anchorage teems with immigrants and refugees of all stripes, all embracing the Great Land, sinking into the Wild, away from the oppression they once knew. Here we joined with those others. We live and work and write together. Our voices, formerly silenced, now mingle to perhaps find healing in our new home.

Land Acknowledgment

THE CITY OF ANCHORAGE, indeed the entire state of Alaska and most of the United States was built on lands belonging to Indigenous Native Americans. Anchorage is the homeland of the Dena'ina Athabascans. In Alaska and across the U.S., Indigenous Peoples were evicted from their lands so that settlers could take over. They were exiled long before I was, and I acknowledge my position as a squatter on their property. We're trying to take care of the place, but those folks did a much better job.

INVOCATION OF THE EXILE

Come now, wanderer, can you stand gazing
Silent while tragic shooting stars quicken your pulse,

As pale reeds rustle at your ankles, and
Fairy beams glitter from frosted habit?

Winds from Western wilds strum the alders to tune
The darkness as your hair dances in time.

Draw near, oh spirit, and lift your nimble voice
To the smiling one who receives your song.

LINES FROM THE EXILE

1. ALONE IN THE CROWD

. . . in which social isolation takes many forms,
despite the maddening hordes.

THE SCARECROW POEM

Your scarecrows
go hallooooo to the
    news. They got
that moldy hay stuffed
  all in their legs.
    It's like arthritis
       and they howl at
          it too:
       Hallooooooo!

CROWS AND COWS

Among the corn, in the
    sullen blaze of morning,
        were crows.
Blasted rows and smoking hulls
    held their gaze as fire swept
        away both food and farmer.
A crash caused the crows to
    leap skyward.
        Came the dawn:
The cows had broken
    the fence to survey the harm—
        ruminating—
They mulled over changes.
    Dim animal minds met,
        a solemn pact was set.
The bell-cow looked up,
    considered assets,
        smelling bassets shadowed in smoke.
"Move," she said, and,
    perched upon their backs,
        the crows rode out with the cows.

Silence is Not a Cat

(Terribly sorry, C.S.)

The cat springs
on typewriter feet.
It sits mewing at
traffic after crashing
a vase with unseen subterfuge
and licks its guilty paws.

Lines before Alexander

The world has changed—
My youthful eyes
see skies of rain.
I know the calm after sobs of pain.
The rhythm of life now rearranged
by the cry of creation or the
sting of disdain.
Ten seconds ago I was young,
now I hold youth in my hands.
I am Fate, I am a god, a king, a man.

Anonymous

Winter has come to my home
And you stand wrapped in cotton,
Swaying in the
Florida breeze looking
At the Cyprus trees,
Thoughts of spreading
Calm alone.

But the chill stiffens
In subtle tones;
Amid the needles brown
We stroll through the
Bracken and quicken at
A sort of sound,
For melting mildly in
The clearing, we find
A baby.

Community Jam

The powers that be turned the cranks
And gears of compression on the freeway,
And at night, amidst the skulking thunderers,
Bawdy tourists, and the odd student
Returning to University,
Each shrugged to a reluctant halt,
Any festivity of the past holiday extinguished
Like a snuffed engine starved for fuel.
Invisible speculations of cause
And curses to cure turned the cold
Air bluer, and it seemed that many passengers
Resented this interstate detainment, whatever its reason.
Patience waned as bladders filled until finally
The click and creak of embarrassed doors opened
To reveal peering faces darkened by shadow,
Silhouetted by headlights and the fog of breath.
A road conceals humanity in its
Hurry to go, yet here, where go is gone,
Humanity crept out to discover itself.
Impatient allies called truce on travel.
The festive atmosphere rose spirits,
Community filled gaps between bumpers and doors,
Offering a seat and a welcome to all,
Sheathed in starlight, a haven from the chaos
Up the road and deep within,
Sustained by huddled, unrehearsed chatter.
Complaining, laughter, all equal here,
Circumstance knit a black band of cheer.

Soon bad news passed down the
Line of tenants in the horizontal high rise:
Eviction; accident ahead finally clear.
The carnival dissolved almost
Instantly as apartments turned to cars once more,

And the timid souls returned to tin machines,
Realizing with shock how exposed they had been.
Again friends became engines, neighbors competitors,
As the race resumed, leaving me to
Contemplate the loss:
A society bred freedom's dross.

Apparition

First, it appears, just a leaf on a tree
A skinny katydid,
Ambling,
Cautious,
Crafty in his camouflage,
Why, surely danger designed thee!
Creeps on stilt legs through the sycamore canopy to safety.

Next, nodding off, in an idle moment, came a vision:
A grasshopper all in blue . . . arrayed on a plate
For a meal,
A buffet,
A feast
Blackened by the griddle and of no use at all.
None would eat normal, much less blue:
Betrayed by aberrancy to land skidding in disaster.

PRIDE

It's a lovely hall peopled
By but one stainless steel
  Watercooler—popular of a sort—
  But another waits around the corner.

He thinks he's the only one
In the world—the sole watercooler—
  And that everyone comes to him.
At the corner, you can see both
  Him and the next one,
But he can't see . . .
  He thinks he's the only one.

MIXERLAND

Life inside a cement mixer is gray—
The wet cement blending with elder generations
Caked against walls, which, here and there,
Show rusting rivets and black stains near an
O-ring where oil has seeped.
Only one way out to escape corruption,
But escape means to be poured and to harden into floors,
And for those of us mixing and spinning inside,
We cannot tell if this truth is a lie.

AN ENTERTAINMENT

Last night I was entertaining thoughts of suicide;
I invited them in to sit on my couch, offering
Pretzels and a movie perhaps,
Lulling them to sleep until, bloated and content,
I threaded the rafters and hanged my thoughts
Upon their own jibs.

At Any Rate

There she is,
this time, the word "pillow"
scrawled with green felt-tip marker
down the edge of her hand . . .
perhaps that's what
she thinks it is . . .
or what she uses it for . . .
      At any rate.

GEN-Z

Daedalus got you all at birth,
Born in a labyrinth with walls of ones and zeros,
And the Minotaur prowls the halls at random.
You got used to the frequent lashings of his tongue,
Even liked them several times
To feel important . . . or in control.

What will you do when you find the architect,
Dead in a corner, skeleton showing
All the signs of being hacked to death by Russians?

NIGHTSHADE AS AN OPIATE

They were fleshy lumps, the children,
Hanging drooping jowls over windowpanes.
Pale cheeks never see
The sun in this land, they flush red
At the hint of movement. Dawn,
Far too taxing, most avoid, choosing
Instead to stay closed right through.
Gone is the warrior shade
Etched in every hallow, for hallows
Rise from hills, rolling and quaking,
And hills are hard to climb.
Were those champions to see their progeny
All would be tempered for combat.
But enlightened children have no
Use for battle; inertia governs morality,
And the human race takes a shortcut
On the path of least resistance,
Which sadly runs to ruin.

LANDLUBBER

Ladies and gentlemen, a sailor.
Judge, if you will, his swarthy skin,
Lined and thickened from
Sun-tanned years.
Peruse his history of port
Travel, his patronage of
Faring Pubs and long line of barmaids.

Note the livery:
His honor bedecked in
Starched white pantaloons,
Blue kerchief and linen cap.
Note, yet, a chevron
On the sleeve to signify his rank
As ensign or skipper.

On his shelf we find Stevenson,
Melville, Coleridge, and Kipling
His heroes: Ulysses and Raleigh;
Farragut and Togo.

Give rope; witness his peerless knots.
In his arsenal is the sheepshank
And . . . several others. Chords
That stamp his every fiber—Sailor.

As he walks, watch him swagger and carry a
Pistol and spot a clipper ship at
Thirty leagues. Marvel at his salty tales,
Descriptions of mizzen masts and scallywags.
He has a parrot named Fishbein.
He is, ladies and gentlemen,
Rough and ready and swarthy.
Truly, here be your sailor.
Hats off, Three cheers, and Land ho!

2. St. Helena

. . . on which Napoleon waits alone for a revolution that will never happen.

The Artist in her Exile

"We must stand apart, for we are not
Purveyors of self or gain in terms of art.
Selfless must not even use 'We,'
And shun all forms of negativity . . .
But directives serve artifice poorly."

    .   .   .

She admires the words of truth and beauty.
There in a dark corner, firmly clutching
Her mind as her only possession,
She may be heard murmuring praise to
No One. Hers is not a call to run races
Or fly oceans to appear before starving
Brown bodies. Hers is from within
As it pours onto the page
Like an upturned inkwell.
A calm wisdom churns her brow,
Yet within she knows wisdom is not hers,
Unshackled from any mimicry of duty
In her search.

    .   .   .

This search stretches along a
Highway that both Socrates and Saviors
Have trod. She has gazed upon the Holy rood
With blasphemous respect. Truth
Is not her exploitation and her
Still small voice imitates
Its owner. She who has ears

Let her hear; she who has scorn—however
Severe—let it sear.
And if her art grows faded,
As the shadows lighten with the
Approach of dawn, it is not the
Time-Shadows which perish her truth[1]
But the approach of the revealer,
The cave opener, the eternal youth
Of Beauty born, and therefore, free.

1. Carlyle

SINE ARTE POETICA

Poetry! despicable distraction
   With its blue and pink pastel flowers:
No scrutiny at all and they prove plastic.
   Why shame me into rhymes
When the masters spoke filth?
   Shelley was a prig,
Tennyson, a drunk,
   Elliot a hazard old man,
   A burning gut full of kerosene.
The leaves of grass are putrid,
   Rude like a lawnmower.
You who sing-song through words
Embarrass yourselves,
   Should be banished with the gypsies,
Your fiddles broken, mandolin strings wound round
Your scribbling digits.
    Maybe the earth
Will blossom with poetry's
   Broken body decomposing
Beneath it.
   Then will fuming nonsense,
This nausea sickening everywhere!
   Be of some small use.

TRUTH AND BEAUTY

    She hates the poem.
Could you read it again?
    She doesn't understand.
We should struggle with this.
    She says she loves the poem.
Is wisdom really a she?
    But I am the poem,
    And I will always be.

SUNRISE: EMPTY MUSEUM

Sunsets scatter diamonds on the beach:
       Free to all most any day,
But a sunrise keeps its treasures closer.
You'll not find folks crowded around
The shore like crabs on a carcass
To breathe the early morning vapors.
Awake and asleep at once, we stare
Into our murky morning coffee
And think of work and carpools and
       Rage at the necessity of both
While the sunrise blazes overhead
Like a child with a picture desperately
Trying to catch an indifferent mother's attention;
       She whimpers off, limping from
       A crippled pride, only to try again tomorrow.

Terror and awe share kinship with the sunrise,
Blazing in mock anger
At patrons who despise her art,
Painted for no one
       And painted for all.
Yet every morning, still dark,
The Artist awakens, chooses brushes, palettes,
       And location
To capture beauty for the sake of letting her go,
       But no one looks, and no one knows.

None stare and sip cappuccino in this gallery,
       But that is nothing to the Artist who earns no salary
For the paint that daily bleeds and fades to sky-blue canvas.
       And the painting serves its purpose only
Because No one stares.
         But what is that? And who cares,
For she does not paint for them.

She paints for those who wish for truth
        To hide the nakedness of their youth
And possess, for a moment, ephemeral beauty
        To give it away as the Artist does.
True Freedom is the possession of release,
Only those who do not seek the gift
        Receive one,
For the giving makes it theirs.

And that is why, this morning,
        The museum of sunrise stood empty,
For none could afford admission.

Titans

The clearness of space can confuse. Beware of devils
In satellites, crusted with ice in a membrane
Like sin. These are the gas giants, remote controllers,
Kindred with the Nephilim:

The rings around his eyes have spun faster today,
Spreading the dust, meteorites scattered from the
Stones he eats, enchanting the pagan in his
Dark pagan keep.

Resinous thorns collect 'round stalk and bean, and Jack
Slips from the weight of gold pulling him home.
He stands to gain from escaping this supper of eggs
And flour milled from bones.

In Jewry, Goliat' plied his weighty dart against the
Puny forces of Good. David stopped him cold in a
Centrifugal discharge of stone upon flesh by planting
A rock knee deep in his neck.

White Star glory purged by larger and whiter
Sank the dreams of Harland and Wolff.
Steel on ice shook planet-sized breath,
Its strength merely humbled its makers to death.

Sofia Tolstoy is proofreading again. She gyres
And gimbles, she circles and grins. But illiterate Goliath
Does not mock, and Saturn can't swallow these seraphim
As she reads through the book and starts over again.

Teaching English at the Asylum

When we walked toward the vague
Building marked with ivy and a
Cryptic oak, my companion committed
To entry. I was guilty, obviously, for
What I'd done to the fool, cramming all
Those letters into his under-inflated mind.
Then like a gear-spring toy, a guard
Popped out of his cube—paranoid perhaps—
Saying to us, "Well, I know him, but I don't know
You!" To avoid a leveled club, I turned
Back to the main wing and checked myself in.
Because I suddenly realized that my whole life
Screamed to see what was inside that vague building.

IVAN THE SCHOOLMASTER

Schoolgirls swarmed, buzzing about the smarmy yard
As if the muskeg had produced an instant infestation.
Outside in the semi-cold, smoke choked the throats of the youngsters,
All afflicted with asthma and sucking on inhalers besmirched with petro-
leum jelly.
Yet indoors, watching, cold reaching fingers to kill, schoolmaster Ivan
Mumbled crumbs of pilot bread into his mouth, swollen and pale,
Drooling with the desire to investigate asthma.
The old goats minding the kids gallop, and they watch, and they gallop,
But on culture camp days, Ivan sits inside and watches and damns the old
goats.

As a boy, Ivan held promise, hid misshapen quirks,
Kind to the ladies and polite with his auntie.
But fate forked his reason, an Ichabod, and now he waits for his moment,
In the upstairs window alone, he scribbles free verse in a sketchbook meant
for pastels,
His own rubbed off long ago to expose harsh, black steel beneath
A reaching, cold spirit.

Miserly Ivan, his thoughts constantly drawn to asthma,
Shuffles out to ring the bell as the children, mostly girls, giggle
At the crumbs of bread left behind on his whiskers.
Rather like Pavlov and rather like Nabokov, the dirty beast rings the bell
And once more drools.

The Magnificent Monster Snake Man

Imagine so void a trade:
to own a semi, a killer paint job,
and a reticulated python ten yards long.

I travel from Wal-Mart to Wal-Mart,
occasionally a fairground,
where, when it doesn't rain, I sit in the
parking lot and let muddy
children and suspicious
parents through the leather flap
and into the aluminum frame
to see Solomon,
all for a buck!

And a man with a pipe in a
tweed suit passes by and stares
through intellectual spectacles;
the college kids glance silently
at my apathy;
the rich women look without looking
and park their Lincolns on the other side
of the lot.

My only customers are grubby boys
and farmers with pick-ups,
and the money I make just pays for
the gas to the
next gig. Occasionally, a bum from
the woods creeps up and sneaks
in without paying.

But I'm not strapped to a Lincoln or
some crummy school. I feed and
manage a snake named Solomon

who can swallow a gazelle whole.
It's a cheap carnival attraction
for a cheap carnival world. And I'm strapped to
that. So, yeah, when the chance
arises, I let the bums in for free.

"I knew him, Horatio . . . "

Yorick planted a skull
In his garden:
>> That of his brother
>> Who died at war.
Yorick's mother wept for
The dead, for freedom,
>> And washed Yorick's hands
>> Of the dirt from the head.
Just this totem was left
As war's reward
>> And Yorick was left,
>> The only of several
Sons never returned.
The father's broadsword
>> Now rusts away
>> In the murky pond
By which Yorick swore
To his mother an oath to avenge
>> And to the feudal lord
>> Marched with a glare and a cringe.
But from afar the lord
Saw and sallied his men:
>> Slayed Yorick in blood
>> And stayed his revenge.
Heroes do deeds
That songs never tell,
>> So Yorick's skull
>> Got planted as well.

After Eight Months . . .

Fazli wrecked his car;
since it wasn't paid off, he still
owes on the loan. Laughing, we asked
if he needed a ride.
But this, he says, is not his trouble.

He walks to work now and
drinks only milk for lunch
(to cut expenses). The mechanics
on his shift offered to help,
assuming limited funds.
But, no, thanks, he says; that is not his burden.

We noticed that he hates the color green,
kicks trees and scuffs turf,
and he flinches at the sight of blood—
faints dead away at a scratch.
We thought maybe he was crazy
or something.

And now he rails against
healthcare (a "parasite
vulture"), and
no one knew why Fazli
smoked so much,
or why he cried behind
the garage on his breaks.

Then we overheard him, one day,
on the phone behind the shop,
cursing at the wretchedness
that would allow a woman
to suffer labor
for a child already
dead.

This was pain atop pain,
a fickle switchback;
a gift of rotten fruit,
a lock on a house burnt down;
a rewritten score.

So we don't bother Fazli anymore.

It is a Thing for Camel's Legs

Not far into the desert, where
Shrubs squint shriveled in sand,
Is a thing not of beauty,
But of love.

No castles piled in heaps nor
Cisterns hidden in dust
Ever held this keening nightmare
Of matted hair and longish face;

Of padded foot and sand-caked eyes,
She hairy be, from waste to heel
And saddened by her thirsty stride:
A hump to burden her spine of steel.

Forsaken she brought misery
To her animal shape with
Feet and legs, slender and tan,
Long like the Arabian *gamalim*,

For dust was her food and doom
Her fate to walk
Her ambling stride
In hope an oasis
Would bubble and form.

She searched forlorn,
Her demon, camel curse
Of hideous compassion,
Destitute charity.

Water was least
Her worry; rather her quest
To seek, to find, to hide,
Without end.

I met her once in caravan
With Bedouins on
Sapphire oasis of
Cooling water. She stood at
An imaginary gate and
Keened sweetly at the morn.

I was not the love she sought
(Came he ever,
I never knew), but my interview
Was lonely like her despair.

"This form is sufficient;
My search is broad,"
She swore,
"But for love, I am undone."
I asked, "Why the desert?
Why reduced to pursue
Love in a form that begs?"

"It is," she replied, "A thing for camel's legs."

WHEN . . .

When Ava sings
feathered notes flutter
about her jungletreehouse room
and fairy wings lift our
feet to salty seafaring nights.

When Ava cries
dearly departed spooks spill
sobbing and blubbering over
every kickingandscreaming surface
while we duck beneath heavy
blockades of sound.

THESEUS STATEMENT

He lays snorting, halved in his humanity
Lungs a bellows of steam
From the dark, boiling broth of his soul.
I am come that he may see that gleam,
The toss of shining truth ringed like
Slabs of a tholos with the honesty of death:
"O virgin eater," I say, "Awake and lift your
Risky head and shaggy hoar;
Roll over as one eye stares, the other fears!"
He pants, he writhes and stands,
Beaded moisture streams like worms
Down his face and curving back.
With a thrust of javelin horns,
His animal fires grow in a rage
That stirs my soul to weep for fear.
Yet his humanity weeps as well,
And I have come to quell his pain
As a tortured mongrel begs for death.
The man within this creature's brain
Anticipates the kill and stills his steaming breath.
All at once, the Minotaur howls as the
Bull regains control—
Of the fear which links his soul to mine—
And he rushes: one great claw of hate.
Unprepared for my greeting,
The man inside curls up beneath the feeling,
Ungrateful in the face of freedom.
I stare with one eye, fear with the other
And lift my pig iron high.
The maze has me trapped, but the creature
Is he who dies. A whiff of sulfur
Clings to the labyrinth walls
As blood streams from a human heart,
And the Minotaur, he falls.

Arabesque on a Persian Rug

For a Student

Behold! These tangled weeds beseech the air
Alone and ebb in swirls of anguished gold.
Within, a peach, a pomegranate stare
From amber coats, or lapis, faded, old.
No rag, no spine less dignified than thee,
Thy swirls and lines upon the floor or shelf
Of mosque, museum, or church—hallow all three
To stare within is to stare at thyself.
Orchard ripened with eloquence and years
Of labor woven in hard-won tendrils
Curving through minds and colors teeming here
And there with insight, fear, and iron will.
Go forth, survive, and weave the fractal fruit
To burn through maze of darkness and of truth.

3. Schism

... in which the reality of systemic racism
causes a rift with the comfortably supreme.

Christopher Columbus in an Omnibus

Columbus wouldn't leave these doors.
Instead, he examined rails and floors and woodwork
    (this being an older omnibus).
The old Italian stayed so long, eventually he
Got promoted from passenger to driver;
      He wouldn't drive though . . .
          Wasn't he the great explorer
            Columbus,
               after all?

ARCHITECT

Concrete blocks and stone,
      he built a corner just off the road,
An incongruous little construction
      of one right angle and a roof.
He fled to a field
      where wildflowers cast shadows at noon,
And there, crunched in his corner,
      he denies growth,
Spreading ignorance like butter
      on a mind like toast.
He built a corner as cars whizzed by,
      clear and streaked like the blurry icicles and
Plums of a finger painting child.
      he built a corner and there he stays,
Out of sight and out of the way.

A Cowrie, Glued to a Magnet

My kid crafted this thing in school today
She taking joy in the pride of her hands.
Quite a value it is to her, yet
To itself, from the far Saharan shore,
An exile, an export, degraded from
Glorious legal tender now
To be propped and stuck and grinning
On my fridge.

Oh make a wish to be, to be
In Africa again.
And buy a field or battle prize
Gaze your imaginary eyes on Empires
Lost and fortunes gained
Now distilled and parodied
As a child's plaything stuck and grinning
On my fridge.

Response to an Editorial

I read your article.
It was like eating a bowl of chicken-bone-marrow:
Full of painful, jagged shards and precious
Little meat. What you forgot,
In praise of your own deserving,
Were the lives crushed out all in one serving.
Now you sound like one whose
Well-wishing sent him to prison—solitary
Wisdom, alone like a whale shark:
Skin all parasites and no friends—
Companions all and none deserving.
You give the sense of an elder fellow,
Beard white, in a crowd, and forgot
To wipe his chin—people staring
Dumbfounded, waiting for the laughter
To begin. And you don't feel the
Crush of eyes, the bitter shame that
Epiphany brings, for, while tossing
Bones to supremacist cousins, you let your face
Reflect their reign.

Pig Men

The pig men come swarming
Down from their high altitude huts
To perform seaside rituals in the fires.
They stand askance on cloven feet
With their beards and broken spears,
Filthied as pig men are in colors
That match their inner stains.
Imported overseas, the ritual shades spread.
These are the lords who shaped a nation
And organized others by pigmentation.

You Wanna Live North

They came like ravens come
  to steal corn from our cribs,
Entered my store with
  them shoplifter eyes, and
I followed 'em like the leash
  follows a dog.
One turned to me and said with
  that big wide mouth,
"Where c'n a fella git a house
  'round hyeah?"
But these people all know
  that we live in Parkside,
So I saw right through
  his clever gimmick.
I drew on my best smile,
  the one I use with my kids,
And I said to that boy,
  "Well, sir, you'll want
To run over to downtown, any
  street between seventh and fourth,
'Cause the places around here
  are all run down,
So, yeah, you'll wanna live North."

WHITE TURKEYS

White turkeys flying down the highway
take a bump and squawk and feathers fly everywhere.
Complaints at the crowded conditions abound,
   "Pardon my snood." "Remove your foot
from my beak, if you please."
   "Alas, there is no room to preen."
White turkeys jammed in crates,
tongues panting, necks jerking, prepare
Their gorgeously filthy plumage for plucking,
Bob their hideously handsome faces for
   beheading, crammed one-two-three,
self-possessed, not self-aware.
I pity them for they are me.
   The truck lags behind as its
crowded purity loves itself in unison,
unaware that bad living conditions
are about to become worse.

The Fall of Man

I encountered skydivers on my evening stroll.
Most fluttered to the ground safely:
Part mushroom and part butterfly.
One, however, staged a revolution. He claimed
Oppression from his burden and,
As he flew, freed himself of his bonds.
The patriot rolled and twisted, head over heels
In rapturous gyrations, his voice shouting hymns
In praise of individualism and liberty . . .
And the likewise-liberated Earth
Rushed forward ecstatically to greet him.
Upon my encounter, there was one less diver.

AN AMERICAN LOOKS AT ANOTHER WORLD

Blank and copper-colored earth blends with
Brown bodies in a barid, arid neverness.
If we feel innocent,
Then innocence is a skeleton—
Bleached like the bodies you know best
   (still a skeleton).
Flies and filth—but no humanity—
Traipse and lapse across screens and
Books and everywhere, except reality.
You can say, you know, it's bad—
But is that humanity in your head
Or Dark mannequins—primitive puppets
Tortured and starved by a landscape
So bare it barely exists—
Patronized and exploited by a
Machine less human than they—
Out-moneyed by a people less
People than they?
Ours is a darker brain
   in a white head.
My definition of humanity, you say,
Does not include deformity, or decay.
If they live they are as you. It's just too
Hot; the problem will go away.
Yeah, verily—because now they're
Not human, not primitive,
Just gone.

4. Refugee

... in which seeking solace in Nature backfires as
the apocalypse of climate change takes its toll.

WHY DID YOU CLIMB THAT TREE?

Oh, was this a tower from Babylon days,
Maybe a linguistic exercise,
A cup of confusion awaiting at the summit?

Perhaps for the thrill of conquest,
Bare feet my sled dogs,
The trunk my solitary North Pole?

Certainly, I saw my princess awaiting,
Imprisoned, cloistered, piping for deliverance,
And mounting the danger, I scaled the castle walls.

Better a grail and I the knight
Grasping gold and encrusted jewels
Reaching out to eternal life after fighting one last infidel!

No mean spiritual ascent,
A Jacob's ladder of illumination
Hoisting me, shimmy-shally, to the nose of God.

A coarse, agnostic, treadmill perchance,
Smoothing my supple flesh to ripples of strength,
A pragmatic callisthenic impractically encumbered?

No, my dears. All quite metaphorical, that,
Yet useless like a glass sponge, since
These lines to be, needed only this tree.

44

Bike Ride on a Flooded Forest Trail

We stood with glassy tin soldier eyes
At a trail that fluttered off a ways.
The flooded pond surrounded the old
Pump house which slumped in the stagnant
Current like an incontinent old man awakened
From a confusing sleep. The dust of
Its timbers mingled with the
Pollen on the wind.
Through these our trail plunged as
The circus of Live Oaks stood posed
Through our pause: a testimony
To nature's mockery at man's
Indecision. The old growth cartwheeled
At our presence with elephant gray
Legs ashen at rough and hollow
Angles—stared us down with the
Sternest of stares—a humiliating
Chorus from the silent keepers
Of the flooded duck pond.
Our tension crested and one
Hesitantly thrust a wheel through
The spongy moss-scum and splashed
Through, a soggy birth for
Two overdue pilgrims, as our
Patron the pump house groggily
Slouched further at his ineffectiveness
To control the flood.
And out we spat free spirits
On the promenade of fronds
Spanning gothic arches with
Magnolia clowns framing spring
Picnic parks and secret hideouts.
With grotesque mallards quacking,
Like frightened monks, a cadence

Of chastisement at our disturbance.
With every turn of our pedals,
We rounded views veiled by
Elders bearded in tangled moss
And sought approval from fence posts
To jump the trail and explore an open field.
Our primeval resonance bemused
The clowns behind, who tuned
The sun to our fancy, an amusement
For small boys maturing in
Such ancient and venerable climes.
And in the faerie light, we sank,
Tired and creaking, defeated by
The adventure, until the wind
Whistled through that merry day
When we were born together in
A clearing; lost alone in the
Shaded bog.

Tylwyth Teg

Emerson and Emily danced arm in arm
   On the frost lawn—fair sprites were they with
He in tails of ebon, she in coats of white.

They twirled upon the hedges,
   A stage of hawthorn wood—staves of fantasy in
Black loafers for him, lily slippers for her.

Then they let in the wind to patter its spry
   Spell upon the window field—sugared crystals with
He in dark-rimmed specs, she with diamond lenses.

As king and queen of blades and beads
   Of dew, they shimmered in silhouetted departure:
He with a long shadow on a hill, she with Harvest moonbeams,

And stumbled down to the front gate of the mill,
   As stars awoke and blinked in Mother Moon's smiling face,
With a black onyx cane for him, spider's silk parasol for her.

To bed, to bed, they lowered the children by fire-
   Light; sleep of glowing warmth under hand-stitched
Sable blankets for him, lace-trimmed quilts for her.

Spring Maiden

Cold and rotten goes fresh and green
Amazing to witness the
Unobservable;
Its growth as fine as evaporation
To sprout lilies after a week of frost.

The woodcutter returns with
A mud of slush and earth on
Leather boots; his axe dull
From ironwood all day.
From freezing to May
Is the breath of the spring,
Angry again like a maiden:

Fair this day
Too polar that,
It is fickle, the season,
Fated to fall to earth;
To be trod upon by winter,
To surrender to the greenish heat
And haze of cicada summer.

Yet winter's aubade
She sings. Powerful fragility
Spun on butterfly wings.
Her tooth is the storm,
Her anger, her rage
At the sap rising slowly up
And out in death.
She is a meadowlark, beautiful,
But caged.

THE SYLVAN

As a child, the
forest had always
harassed. Now
homeless, the Great
Mother beckons, though
at night she still
fears.

By day, she
lives with hemlock
sap and canned
yams. At night
she crouches,
drinking
tears.

In the timberland unknown
bits of iron
wood, and stone, there
she lived alone
for
years.

An Earthworm Aristotle

Three years have passed and still I've yet
to pen the outpouring all in one week
that brought gasping the prophets
to my muddy feet.

It was a muck time when squiggles
and theorems crowded the sidewalk
in a bird-dream Mensa convention
where I met Aristotle.

The thoughts that the old wiser
could tell if not for his writhing
and gasping in a puddle of silt
would fill several more volumes of Physics.

He bore witness to his rigid
changefulness, as wind blew leaves,
rain soaked philosophers,
and I pounded through the broth.

His slick-skinned form fermented those
minds nearby and what of this usefulness
or the deft effulgence of nature
to creep slowly on that gray horizon?

This was a withering time for earthen comedy
to wring a comely pattern of
chaos from those sandy loins
as dank and repulsive as Cyclops.

For as I stood staring,
Aristotle split his side and
memories crept swimming into
the miry millions of peers.

He went calmly to his fate,
setting an example to top Socrates,
surrounded by disciples all
burbling his name.

And I resumed my walk to the
post office, deftly stepping
over Menander and Euclid
as I trod.

August Ablaze

For the climate refugee

There were no poems this summer.
The fear was too hot to run slick for
speech. The rhymes popped and the
meter blew, and those who had feet
grew wheels. There were no poems
this summer as flames grew,
and zephyrs carried the storm home.
Away from the mountains and the Autumn
oracles, no poems in August
for hurricanes in the jungle to ruin.

Vehicular Homicide

Come dawn, most crooks pause,
Sleepy still, and lazy in their beds.
But I revved down the road
And gained the turn with illicit eyes,
Innocent but unwise, like a toddler with a stolen pie.
My target, a robin, stalked me, matching my speed,
And I attacked with a robbing thud,
Watching behind me as the victim flailed.

Passing later, I saw it there,
Calm eye set in a tragic stare,
A meaningful model of hopeless patience,
To be flattened by subsequent felons.

FLORIDA FIGHTING CONCH

We used to collect seashells;
We'd scrub the knuckles of our toes
Into the sandy silt of Sanibel's beaches
Sifting out kitten paws from the
Multitude of ponderous arks, occasionally
Reveling in a lettered olive, its
Perfect smoothness almost
Irrational in this gritty context.

But the real prize was the
Florida Fighting Conch.
Sturdy shells with spikes rusted like
Dried blood, they were the
Stoutest of the rarities.
And surprise! They were
Sometimes alive.

That's where they get their name,
If you caught one alive, it fought—
Ramming its siphon into the soil,
The conch could leap twice its body length
Attempting to escape. They didn't fight us.
Or each other.
They fought for dear life.

But it's illegal to take them
Alive. Death sentence to aerate
A gill breather like that.
So we collected the dead ones.
Bodies rotted away and beautiful
Exoskeletons remained.

Then I realized. My collection,
Its grizzly reality affixed, on display
In warm colors and tightly-
Printed labels,
Was a shameful shrine to store.
We don't collect seashells anymore.

No Remedy but the Sun

This frozen(shaded)frightening(violent)
world will always
win
By grinding away, sharp or dull,
Diminish gradually,
Weak or strong, smart or dumb,
You have no remedy but the Sun.

Under cover of night(crime)silence(rape)
The culprit gets away
a traitor
to truth
Wraps you in bindings of time.
Its shame keeps you on the run
With no remedy but the Sun.

A stockpile, made by hands(sweat)slavery(death)
no good
to anyone,
But still you pack it up and ship it
To the States
To be bought by everyone.
It leaves no remedy but the Sun.

RUNNING OUT OF STONE

Sift through the crust
and rummage down—fill in gravel
pits—and chisel smooth the mountains
then, you'll see,
once we're out of stone,
these piles of plastic tucked
behind every town will seem so
Picturesque.

NOTES ON A HOMESTEAD MIDDEN, SEWARD, AK

Step softly through the moss; the spongy
Mass deceives. Sharp edges hide.
Scrape away the duff to find a coffee tin
Or Mason jar peeping from spruce needles
Shaded by salmonberry.

The folks on the knoll used the slope
As their landfill four score years ago,
Yet note how lush the landscape lives:
Cottonwood sent knuckled roots into the loam
Fortified with iron oxide from rusting nails,
Fungi crumbled timbers with hyphae fingers.

How can we call this pollution? Pioneers left
Behind fertilizer, not pestilence. The clean
Artifacts of stone, steel, and bone tell
The story of the past while growing the future.

Not so our reeking hills of toxic filth,
Trinkets and chemical spills blight
The land, kill for centuries. How did
We shift from crafters to destroyers?
Helpless in our homes so that factory
Fumes can belch out cheap solutions
To unimportant problems.

An Earthworm Exodus

thunderstorm,
and earthworms pour by the thousands across
a flooded sidewalk
uncertain if they are Israelites
or Egyptians.

5. Exodus

... in which scandal and doubt erode the once-safe haven of religious belief.

The Rebellion of Korah

You have gone too far! You who stand
In divine robes and clothe your own brother
With holiness while we eat manna and sand
Every day and must hear only, never bother
His holiness with the oh-so-radiant face!
We do not believe that the Lord has appeared
To you or anyone else. Here, we defy
Your leadership; we have feared
You long Enough!

My face is scarred by rubbing ash from my eyes,
My hands burnt from handling seared flesh.
Never have I been inside this tabernacle, yet I
Serve outside blindly! We who escaped one mesh
Of lies to land in a prettier net, ours perhaps, but poor
And under-fed! My cattle are skin, their bleating
Pitiful in my ears at night. We must use spoors
For cookfires since acacia is scarce. Bleeding
Altars rule our lives, and my family says Enough!

I have summoned allies, Moses. You may summon whom
You will. You promised us milk and honey,
And so far we have found a desert of fire
And clouds and storm. We will walk your stony
Path no more. I have assembled my brothers, Levites
Of my tribe, against your tabernacle and your Aaron.
We have brought our censors, our incense; the Levites

Will choose the fertile road and depart from the barren,
Even then it is not Enough!

I remember months on Sinai, bearing days of nonsense
As you gamboled in a storm cloud and brought down
Your rock laws. I remember well the bitter penance
You had us drink when Aaron was bent to build the cow.
Did you punish your priest then? But how many thousands
Died in the vengeful plague as your privileged siblings
Quibbled and prospered? Your God's sarcasm is iron bands
That choke and kill! Remember the quail, Moses, dripping
From the sky like hail before we'd had Enough!?

We will no more be slaves to your bloody God! Cattle
And livestock aplenty have been spent when priests
Could all of us be. And we will hear no more Canaan prattle,
For it's back to Egypt with us. Better slaves with yeast
And life than God's with manna and blood and death!
You may write this in your book, "Here Levi claims
The Priesthood and with our censors billow the true breath
Of holiness." And tho' the ground opens and fire rains
From Sheol, we still have had Enough!

The Goblin of Nonesuch

(after reading the Ellesmere MSS)

Shod with a dog of a pig-horse he rides
Jangling a line of dreary toys caked with filth.
Calls them relics, sells to clerics' boys,
Salivates for the clink of coin.

But the likes of him are banned from the Close,
Since the Saracens came to Nonesuch town.
Their domes hunch the horizon like a bent
Old woman, all below them broken and bones.

Alecto he hight, limping his name
Like a gargoyle, staring down stony
Dragons along the hostile town.
Wheezing, disease rides his lungs;
Still he sings, quieter these days.

Door after door, he searches for priests
Who once sponsored his trade. Croaking for
Alms, the priests gave; Saracens give too,
Mostly knocks with their canes. Alecto
Dodges most, takes a few.

Long ago Saracens came, boarding
Up windows and renaming shrines;
They drove the priests underground.
Alecto's crew they dubbed 'goblin,'
Granted a boon: to sing or to swing.

So weary with singing, but left with no voice
The goblin slouches, his hatred subdued.
Broken by priest and Saracen alike,
He waits like the sea for a change in the tide,
Mumbling curses at old masters and new.

AL-AQSA, JERUSALEM, OCTOBER 8, 1990

A murmur mounts as Ijma,
The Muezzin, takes to the stairs.
Though tan and cracked, the stones
Of the tower remain proud and firm,
Reverberating with the echoing
Of sorties and salat centuries old.

The thrumming drives out the heat, past shaded eyes pounding
With religious fervor; the worshippers, drones to outsiders,
Stand free of their sandals, cloaked in white, and chant.

"Praise be to God, the Lord of the Worlds!"
Blasts a twenty-year-old loudspeaker in warbling tones.
The sound waves mimic the shimmering heat:
Cracked voices thirst to partake,
To descend from the mosque as masters.

Into this, Ijma steps down and bows low,
Facing Mecca, Mohammed's own,
Points his nose to the prophet's home,
Then lifts a stone and lets it go.

              .   .   .

Belly up, later, in the soaking sun,
The Mosque stands emptied of life,
Voided and terrifying to passing tourists.
Dust devils billow through her courtyard;
Caretakers mop up the blood.
But still the stones hum with that ringing prayer,
And the sky looms deepest blue there.

Natural Revelation

Have you fathomed the Mystery of silk
From one whose essence imbibes so
Much blood? From this tribunal all
Beauty emanates. From moist and filth
To barely there—the beads of
Dew hovering in air.

Morning fog—with nothing completely
Real—the spirit world but a few breaths away.
Here, specter-like, emanates the midnight creations
Of the black weaver. Suspended between branch
And lead, a cloud more solid lingers to
Disappear with the morn.

In her is the blueprint—the maker's eye—to design
A trap—a thing of beauty—a tool for an assassin
To point so prominently to that Outside Other.
Can this spiraled Mesmer be the mystery of revelation
Hovering in a field of hazy green?

OVERHEARD IN THE SOUTH TRANSEPT

You there, gray boy,
   I see you—barely-there shadow—
On what business . . . what noise to disturb
   The perilous twilight . . .
Came you to this marble thicket?
   Do you seek help for hurts
To heal spirits crushed by cruel parents,
   Mentors—disillusioned seekers hardened
By sex scandals rolled up into gray
   Cardboard tubes shipped overnight
Via Fed-Ex to the FBI?
   What did you think you'd find
Scuffing our already chipped paint to
   Light skinny candles soon to
Diminish in dusky impotency?
   Here, maybe you heard of priceless
Relics and princely gargoyles, triptychs
   And lollipop glass with titillating nudes.
The Parish trustees had these whitewashed and
   Chiseled smooth after the cardinals
Unanimously voted Offendedness a Venial sin,
   And the priests moved that
The increased load at confessional strained
   Their already overwhelming responsibilities.
No, my son, we cannot offer you a handout
   Since the rectory Christmas party is today.
Communicants receiving aid need apply
   On Saturdays with appropriate documentation
As a member in good standing . . . . You must be off, then?
   Very well. I wonder terribly why young
Folk have no reverence for consecrated spaces
   These days.

The Child Life Cardinal Lead

Nobody told me that the Cardinal had
Been at his soap bubbles again.
But, there can be no doubt, the shiny
Slick patina on the closet wall, tinged
With iridescence like a vulgar rainbow
Sliding down a smog-filled thunderhead,
Gave the bald man-child away.
I looked for the tools of his trade
(The fellow could create a cottage industry
Of loafing) and found one slime-bedewed
Wand tucked in a slipper: if he must
Perform the infant's art, must he do it
In the closet?
I finished my ruined rosary—no doubt
God was planning to curse me further—
And stalked through the abbey
To find the white-haired boy
Listening to lullabies in the chapel,
Nodding in innate innocence.
He somehow finds meaning in his
Childish, un-Christian antics.
He knows nothing of propriety, piety, or
Sobriety: opening his censer to watch
The embers burn,
Giggling at a Latin baptism as the
Father stutters when the baby screams,
Reading fairy tales in the bathtub and
Ruining the book by dripping!
The sacristy has become a nursery,
And his antics disturb Holy Communion.
God's grace is not for childish pranks.
I returned to the chamber to retrieve the wand—
Lord knows I should punish him . . . again—
But mercy prevents it.

I resolved to greet him next time,
In Latin, as usual, not that he ever understands;
I have tried treating him as a competent
Component, displaying virtue and compassion
As he pursues his Georgian foolery,
And, oh yes! we suffer: the parish is in shambles;
Paint so old will naturally peel.
Just last week, even, I noticed
Flakes in the Cardinal's own cup . . .
But I don't think he did.

LAMENTATION OF THE STRONGMAN

Sanctuary! Father, these doors
Whose hinges I have bent in my fervor
Must contain. This cloister be my
Bar and God my judge if I leave.
The Saints' white sockets
Pierce my empty hands. This thumb—
Twice yours—quivers at the carols
Of devils and stuffs my ear.
I, Father, stand impaled upon
Iron and anvil—skewered by my
Deeds, pursued by my victims.
God must judge me, Sanctuary!

Mine is the carnival strength,
And my living is made by hoisting
Men on lanyards about the tent like
A sailor who hoists his stock; my hands
Harness the power of the pulleys.
These hands now stained crimson
As carnations on Augustine's grave;
A child have I torn—one child, my blood—
O, Sanctuary! Hounds are at my feet.

Father, while performing, a plot for
My purse arose and during intermission
Executed. Fleeing, the cowards brought
Their boy to see the show and left
Him behind—He tripped upon a rope.
In my blind rage—'twas all they stole—
I gripped the boy and cried,
"Cease or pay for thy theft!"
Cowards! They fled and I bellowed
Bullishly—eyes washed crimson—and tears
Ran down my face. The tears of

A strongman, Father, do they
Not thy heart stir?

Sanctuary! My raving finished, I
Looked down to see the boy dead.
Mercy on the innocents in the arms
Of a strongman. Sanctuary, Father,
Thy walls condemn!

FLAGELLANT

"Blasphemy takes many forms, one of
Which stands before me!" The ostler spit ale
On his apron and leaned back, peace said.
Humphrey glanced at his watch, licked his
Lips, and left the pub, too self-consumed
With the publican's words to remember paying the tab:
    Yet another charge.
"Filth," he murmured and slogged through
The street, muddying his priest's robes,
Shaded like a crow razing a forbidden crop,
Convicted, yet complacent, reluctant to budge.
Time passed and Mass came, absently for
Humphrey, whom it pleased to drink up
Any leftovers and leave his guilt
As a hound slinking home from abuse.
    "Blasphemy,"
The word sagged through Humphrey's veins,
And his mind told him the ostler was insane.
The pub was open to all, Christ beckoned,
He had entered; it was Divinely ordained.
With a fogged mind, the priest fell asleep
And dreamed the verse again
In a restless, singsong metronome:
            Curses that spoiled and spilled the ink
            Make the Virgin Mary stink.
            Lurches and cowls betray the cloth:
            Are Sons of God the Sons of Sloth?
Cold sweat splashed a rapid, lidded eye, and
Humphrey awoke with a start, lilies
At the bedside overturned and water everywhere.
The sewing machine, where the priest
Mended his own collars, beckoned; another calling.
And twenty minutes later Humphrey discovered
He had stitched a bloody seam up his

Left hand. Smiling at the pain
He dressed, careless of the stains,
And walked down cluttered Browning
Street to the pub and went in.
This time, the ostler was not there.

LOCKED OUT OF A CATHEDRAL

Why always I must feel as blind
To sights my brethren see?
                    —*Thomas Hardy*

      Your doors were closed,
A full six years of unmixed emotion rose
And bled away on grounds of godly stone
Where once the honor of your presence gave
Chills of tension to feel with skin and bone
The roses of your panes, your dimming nave,
All when, grieved, I turned away, was froze:
      Your doors were closed.

      You insincere,
Neglect the small through urge to be austere—
I know that mercy lays not upon your halls,
Your grove of columns flagged with sterile views
To praise no Craftsman save the shaper of your walls.
Continue to deceive the pilgrims in your pews,
But you are exposed, and so I leave you here,
      You insincere.

MENDICANT

Sing your lark, Puppetman,
Like a keg with no powder,
A scarecrow with no straw
Awaiting farmer's flames.

Why do you continue from a riddled
Pulpit your hand-copied answers
Faded and frayed from thumbing
For quotations?

Who are you, Puppetman, to stand barefoot
And preach of shoes?
Like a mongrel claiming pedigree,
You praise health in your sickness!

A curse from Moses you are;
Shelomith's son to
Be sanctified by hands and
Sacrificed by stones.

There are strings at your feet,
Ashes and torn by the farmer's blaze;
Your disciples have rioted and gone home,
And you, motionless, remain.

ALL HALLOWS

One warm Halloween night Satan came with glowing blue light
And laid waste to an entire block, just to get to me:
Children in the streets dressed as spooks, calorie bags in tow
But behind, behind, the devil has entered the wood.

Starts with a breeze—wrong direction from real—
And soft glowing leaves steal toward my house,
Careening my way just as All Saints Day
Breaks with the chimes at midnight.
What did I know? Asleep. Peacefully sealed.

Tendrils through the window curled 'round my head.
And the pressure—God!—crushed right in my bed.
Like old Giles Corey in Salem grim
The limbs weighed me down, like boulders, like sin.
"Awake or be dead!" says a voice painted red
But too late. I'm crushed. Fluids from every orifice gush.

But Lo! I survive. Sobbing, awake, to my wife, "I'm alive!"
Blending a version of half-life and death,
Reality tilts with each confused breath.
That outcome, that fear has momentum and mass:
Suspicious forever of each oak that I pass.

Lignum Vitae

      Pomona fought with her
Husband on Tuesday,
Left the house in a rage of ravishing
Thoughts.
Planning revenge, she stormed
To the orchard, determined
To force the season's end.
She grew blind as
The slanting sun pierced
The horizon as it set.
Pausing with a squint,
She turned East and drank in
Verdant wines, bewitched.
And seeing an apple tree
She mounted aloft, swift of foot.
Brushing cicada nymphs aside
(Really agéd Tithonas,
Who never died)
She found apples, golden
Like the Hesperides. And healing
Came to her hands, to hold that
Halcyon fruit.
      Descending, she sought Vertumnus
Once more, determined to
Bring apples as offerings of peace,
But, lo, she looked and saw
From the windfall that few fruits
Had ripened and instead, strewn below,
Open sores and rotten cores reeking with
Neglect—the society of apples in steep decline.
Committed, she picked, saving
As many as she could—reaching and grappling
Those still firm, selecting fruit not infected
By the unseen worm.

Those she gathered engorged her tunic
To maternal fullness, perfecting
Her power to change. As she strolled home,
Dusky skies rosied her cheeks,
And the apples ripened
To full potency, their fragrance
Alerting Vertumnus from afar
So that he awaited her on the doorstep;
She tossed the fruit as she came, wine-dark
Skins to his uplifted hands.

A Prayer for Moderation

"Go into all the world," He says,
And we go, but, one moment, Lord,
Just where?
The world's quite a large space
And, no offense, but you pretty much
Stayed in just one place.
Life is fear to us; we, the chosen
Left fasting in catacombs
Or feasted upon by
Lions or skewered by Trajan.
But where, in the slurry of
Suffering and waiting and worrying
Is the finality, the joy, the lasting
Fullness of a job well-done?
Did we miss it?
Has it not come?
Naturally,
We look to the here, the material.
Lord, you know this, do you hear
Our moans? They are complaints;
We are at best imperfect saints who
Can bear great loads, but, Lord, only
For a season, lest it reach beyond reason.
War is too much.
Peace, too little. Can there
Be, O God, such thing as a middle?

6. Cantos

. . . in which anxiety and loneliness become a kind of hell,
and, like Dante, we take a tour.

Canto I: Downstairs

Downstairs, the dark drips
  over basement appliances.
Downstairs we might get
  away from what is above.
Downstairs you can fall through
  the cracks of your own clumsiness,

Downstairs makes me cough;
  I suppose it's the damp.
Downstairs befriends gravity
  and entropy and inertia.
Downstairs makes upstairs so
  very far away. So difficult to get to.

But you need no directions to get downstairs. All
  you have to do is Fall.

CANTO II: FEVER

Dark murmurs with crystal colors
   Purple heat and marching words,
Clouds in the wind of death and confusion
   And still I sit.
   I wait. I drool a little
   Here on my side.
     No amusement breaks the spell;
     Pennies wasted in a wishing well.

    .   .   .

A daylight brighter than noon seduces senses,
     A traveler trapped, snared by the false orb.
Lives on bread and water
Tasteless, breathless, looking for his daughter
     And for her sake
     And for the thorns on her head
—How many pills did I take tonight?—
     He does not die
     He only burns.
A life of fear of death is hell . . .
     He only burns.

Canto III: A Vision at Burial

Bury me in the ground
headfirst so I can
see into Hell—include
a tube, long and hypodermic,
piercing the skin—worms
and nerves within. Lift my
dead lids, as fluid and grubs
rush to my head.
Unfold for me a
scene from below:
leopardemon stages tearing
scenes, eaglizard stealing
flesh from live carrion,
skinless monks screaming
chanted darkness as souls—
drunk with fear and scarred
by boils—hang from
Haman's gallows.
Watch, oh sunken eye,
these souls. Peer me
into the earth,
show my toes lest they
sprout with almonds—
like Aaron's cane—or my
scope crack in the tomb,
Hades' room, and bury
me, almond free,
         head down.
This body I'm in
has a hole—dug with
shovels and with moles—
eaten to its core to find
soot and shadows—

Famished to skeleton
bones decayed, my eyes
will close on the age
of rage—sown and grown—
head down.

Canto IV: The Song of Sylvester

(verses 1-5)

How beautiful you are my lethargic, slobbering dumpling,
Oh, how beautiful you are!
Your eyes are like cormorants thrashing in curdled pond scum.
Your hair is like a tangle of tapeworms coughed up
from the dregs of a rabid hound.
Your teeth are like a phalanx of rusty staples
protruding from the creaking timbers
of a derelict mineshaft,
And the symphony of their gnashing intones the melody of
shattering glass.
Your lips are like twin sucking leeches,
And your mouth is puckered and pale.
Your temples are like withered orphan conies
starving huddled in blasted pits of sand.
Your neck is like a lonely castle of Ireland,
crumbling granite and creeping moss
with the jawbones of a thousand warriors
swinging sadly from the battlements.
Your two breasts are like lunar crags
laden with peeping craters and scarred rocks
that smoke with acrid fumes.

Canto V: A Molotov Syringe

On condition of your greatness
We invite you to the times,
Tributes, and nonesuch of life.
These are illusory, so watch your step.
For upon your acceptance,
Yes, lots of nice things happen,
But in return, we insert the
Needle and inject fire through
Your veins.

Canto VI: Laurels of the Underworld

Mulberries fall about the indentation where
Steven lays guillotined,
And jays their carols raise to feast.

A crown of figs appears at
Mr. Abbott's head
Fueled with bile, a skulker, a stinker.

The brambles, an alloy of pain,
Shy at the sulfur stench
Of a nameless Ancient, bitter and feeble.

And from Molly the sweetest pears
Nurse from her breast,
They much sweeter than the song of jays.

Canto VII: University of the Damned

Why a cavern for matriculation?
You speak lectures fit to spit roast,
But fat melts at lower than boiling for water,
This I've learned;
My whole graduating class has learned.

"Eternal Torment 101" reads the
Door whose knob burns every
Single damn time,
And the books, unintelligible,
The language of demons.

My sober brothers, we have
Gathered on this festive occasion,
Hydrogen balloons exploding in our ears,
To end it all,
These final moments of the Humanities ball.

Canto VIII: Lethe and Limbo

They came at last to Beulah, well, the River just before,
Each turned to a companion to share the kiss of death.

Hence upon the banks, the waters lapped their chilly toes,
And guilty they perceived descent to a paradise of mortal woes.

And of all, one alone lifted hands and tilted into the plunge
By instinct to escape and let the water fill her lungs.

Those remaining knew only to watch, reluctant to move,
Neither sentenced to reward nor blessed to meet their doom.

And by and by, their fingers, limbs, ears, and all transformed:
Ah, lovelies, such a forest of procrastination on that bank adjourned.

Probably they grew mighty trunks with windy branches shaken
By drowsy, nodding snores in dreams; their quest forsaken.

But she alone braved tide and deep to cross the other side
Continued in forgetfulness, but grateful she had died.

7. Wilderland

. . . in which a literal exile arrives, and we exchange
the heat for a more arctic clime.

Saying Goodbye to People who Never Cared about you in the First Place

That's one less post
one less like
to remove from the list
of longings.

That silence
in your pocket?
That's them not calling.

It's like a funeral,
yours and theirs—
the only together left.

Walled up like
Antigone.
Blockaded like
a Confederate.

Yet no revolution's
flag gives meaning,
no rebellion will justify.

And all that's really lost,
in the end,
is illusion.

Deeper Dell

We climbed in search of game
Higher, deeper past green meadows
Over tumbled scree to ridgelines—
Cleft vales choked with fog.
And maybe the fog waylaid us,
Obscuring, perhaps, the shape
Of our destiny.

Anyhow, it came to pass,
And at the pass we looked down
On unfamiliar turf. Streams
Ran muddy, unfit for drinking.
The last scramble too steep
For return travel. Forward and down,
Our only choice. So on we go.

LIFE OUTSIDE THE AIRLOCK

Grind or ground, like tungsten carbide,
Am I the cutting edge or the exploration?
Giving way to heat and friction
To erode, eventually nothing left,
Unless, perhaps, maybe, a motherlode awaits.

But thrust outside like this,
It seems unlikely. Alone and cold
And pressed on all sides.
An immigrant. An exile. Surrounded,
Sounded, sundered, plumbed.

What is at the core? When will
Atmosphere be restored?
Never is likely. Never is now.
Inside out. Hold hands and
Eyes tight. Tell myself it will be alright.

But right itself has shifted. Amnesia,
Like a dream, waking forgetfulness,
Breath held to withhold the rush of cold,
We can only hold the line so long.
Turning blue. What was I doing?
What did I do?

I Live in Two Towns

I live in two towns
One is white and one is brown
One is up and one is down

One is left and one is right
One is dark and one is bright

One is north and one is south
One is bleeding from the mouth

One is snowy; one is green
One is fat and one is lean
The first secure, the other mean
This one hidden; that one seen

STELLER'S JAY

What hope have we when among our rocks and spruce
Such ghastly shade emerges?
Yet living still, the creature, blue, save
Head and bill, seemed blasted by fire.

Stock still, no fear exhibits,
He lopes about as if showing off
Wounds that must needs kill
A lesser spirit with lesser will.

If thy fate, O fowl, can be thus born,
Then I my burdens bear all the better.
Among bracken and moistened fern
A mate awaits, and young one's food to earn.

Hymn to a Great Land

I toiled to the summit of Wolverine
Sat down and penned this song
Perhaps not at peak performance.
Do not confuse this praise for worship
And hence bring guilt of idolatry.

Yes, as ridgelines march beneath me,
So does pride. Lofty stone on stone—
A henge greater than any Druid's—
Standing ringed and ramped.

Smoke from the valley below
Boils over, pours over as steam
Clears, collects, and repeats,
Change the only constant.

Rising to crest, falling to sea.
Delicate saxifrage, gentle survivor
Covers all. Sustaining berries, streams
Shared by marmot and city alike.

Blank Space

mind at rest
sky clear of clouds
infant sleeping at noon
clean canvass
peace treaty
unexplored frontier
at the edge of the map

WE ARE NOT PATIENT

—a chronicle of South Fork Eagle River Falls

We are not patient.
Look to the rock enjambed
In the tumbling creekbed,
Icy cataract pouring
Down its back
Years to eons.

A bath of moments would
Wind our clocks to zero
Puffing and cramped,
Severe of the chill,
Hysteric at moisture
Or just a stubbed toe.

But who would cry
For the dipper bird
Dancing alone at
The rill? Bobbing
For breakfast
An hour or ten
Catching a nap
To begin again.

But our meals
Are faster,
Our lines short
Lest we stamp
And dance a reel
Of rage.
We are not patient.

Cottonwood leaning
Across the stream
Endures a torrent
Of ages pounding
Bark to slick timber.
A son sees it one day,
A grandson decades later.

Yet the father abstained,
Growing up fast,
Back bent to men's work,
Adolescence dissolved into
Sweat and fear.
So the grandson viewed the cascade
All alone in the rocky glade.

You Know how it is, Mr. Narwhal

Days without end chasing a spike,
You swim to the right, swerve forward again and still it remains
Just out of reach.

You feel those arms bound
Pinned to your side, fingers fixed,
Flippers hardly able to flex flap grasp
Blubber beneath your gunmetal hide.

And that neck! Fused head-to-torso
Stretched tight that mottled skin,
Body won't bend. You've never
Seen your feet. Look down to try and
Oops, you impaled yourself.

Cold water everywhere, caps
Of ice limit your air,
Search for a crack to gasp, you
Punch through with that enervated Spear,
Sending three million needles of pain straight
To the cortex part of your brain.

MORNING CALLER

A solitary fellow in a black cap
and white cowl
Came calling at my window.
Sat upon a birch twig and inquired
of my health.
"Very well!" I said and poured out
The tea, for me alone.

He jittered with the cold and
A mane of snow ringed his crooked
hands.
"I wish I could invite you in," I said.

Alas the pane betwixt us
Keeping me warm and him without.

"No bother," cried he, "Many to see!"
And with a twitch, he vanished
Ruffled not with anger
But to keep close the
Heat within his coat.

Now alone again, I watch the spot
He vacated: a gap in the snow
On a limb.

8. Relegatio[2]

. . . in which we wait patiently, rapt in the identity crisis
of rejection and change.

Sackaversary

What so soon?
Caught in limbo, suspended in glue.

Dig your grave,
A life dissolved, the one you have,

Now at noon.
Widow's window, a glowing blue

Warms her face—
Ghostly dance in a ghostly place.

---

2. The *relegatio* was the Roman Empire's mildest form of exile. Victims kept their property, family, and citizenship, but had to leave the boundaries of the Empire itself.

I do my Crying in my Dreams

I do my crying in my dreams
That way no noise disturbs those
Moaning more heavily than me.

I waste my worries on myself
While those careworn others do
Much more with their lives.

I see the past and destruction
O'ertakes and with closed eyes
Hurtle forward in flight.

I open my hands but close them
Again, no tool nor sword may
Parry the leering flame.

I roll mutely over, belly up,
An oblate to coiled cruelty
Keeping all awake with my weeping.

MEGALOPHOBIA

These terrible towers dizzy me up like nausea
Cresting in tsunamis of green.
Standing in a canyon of glass 900 meters
Veering skyward, clouds make movements huge
And I sink to the sidewalk in forced prostration.

One visit to a dockyard to see a pinnacle
Of impossible steel floating angrily in the sky
Shimmering with threat might
Crush me at any moment from the
Slightest ripple in the sea.

Thus it's always been with the very large,
Palms sweat as huge looms nearer.
Be it tractor or windmill,
Tilting up at these giants
I feel my minish
Like a mite wielding a hair against
An aircraft carrier.

The Titan, whether moon or myth, crushes
Perspective and smashes you into the
Atomic, a mental shrink ray
That dismantles humanity,
Discounts all affections
And threatens to vanish in the
Ever-expanding galactic vast.

There I am, exponentially small
Next to sequoia, skyscraper, mountain, Mars.
Descending rapidly down the scale,
The sharp chords play deadly down my spine.
All is small in the shadow of the supersized.

But maybe it's not true.
Maybe Mars is large
Despite the sun. The sun
Hangs and galaxy be damned.

Looking over our shoulder in our flight from the universe
There's the Earth, that speck
Insignificant seeming,
But not small, no,
Not tiny,
Just far away.

THE EGG

O little oblong orb
we waited like a
stranded tortoise.
Decades alone
a sigh, a glance to the horizon
and down at you.
We paced a furrow in the
sand, sun whirling a horseshoe
dervish, seasons stacked
in heat, snow, sleet, rain
drenched, fingers swollen with
the moisture, another glance down, water
dripping from our noses splashed your
smooth shell.
The bones of turtles past bleached
and crumbled over ages.
Our own skins dried and split,
crushed shells scattered there
and there, an assortment of failures
nosed by oystercatchers and gulls.
We hovered protectively, but
doubts of life crept in.
Were you in there?
Then with blurred vision
our hearts broke. We despaired,
flung ourselves down
with curses at the promise,
now a lie.
Gasping, exhausted, we
gave up. And eye-to-nose
At last, we saw the first opening.

THAT LIGHT YOU SEE

This one time, sat in a cave
Dark, and a drip triggers
Tinnitus

But dark didn't blind
It was the light at the end of
The Tunnel

Bright point
Fiery drill boring
Its threat of heat
Through my iris

Shifted backward
Slid on scree down
A slight incline
And still it chased
Driving deeper

Every direction it
Tracks every
Crystal refracts
With laser intensity

It's the pin in my
Butterfly wings
Anchored to bedrock
An ache that washes
Out all other thought

Leave this cave? To
Be bathed and
Baked? Certain death that
So it's crouch and squint

Squirm and knit
Illuminated and exposed

Winter Morning in an Anchorage Kaladi Bros.

This robe of night fits poorly by morn,
Bunching and gapped from rolling
To find warmth.

Settled to fate, we trudge through
Waking and routine, whittling
Hours and resigned, however S.A.D.

Sitting by the window only mirrors
The room until halfway through
Your first coffee, the shift appears.

Not the dawn, much less the sun,
Still dawdling nearly an hour
Below the horizon.

Instead the gray line of sky
Draws itself behind mountains.
The contrast invisible moments ago.

It's your first glimpse of the stage,
First hint that the curtain will soon
Be drawn.

Few notice, yet pulses quicken,
Voices raise, the depth of field
Widens for the first time today.

And with it comes life, comes
Hope; that horizon you see
Holds the future, made more
Real by that brightening gray.

THE LONELIEST PLACE

We scoured the mariner's map for valleys
On islands segregated by nautical miles,
Perfect hills away from roads, huts, rivers,
Anywhere to get away.

And each drew crowds. Lonely seems
So popular these days. The webcams
Scan an empty horizon and likes
Pour in like acid rain.

Footpaths crisscross St. Matthew
Now, a crushed egg under a boot print
Shows where crews offloaded
Passengers laden with cameras for selfies.

But I'm in midtown, standing in the median
Pelted by gravel kicked up by traffic.
A Yup'ik lies supine in the fog, the only inhabitant
Of this island, his head dangling dangerously
Near the curb. The fog won't clear for hours,
And I'll be gone, knowing that
The tourists all got it wrong.

EXHALATIONS

The gulf exhales, eternal gusts accelerate
Through Resurrection Bay, focus on the
Town their target. And the village groans
Its endurance, timbers pop and siding
Shivers. Sitka spruce up and down the
Slopes twist and creak, showing stress cracks,
And occasionally fall, colliding to their snowy fate
To feed the forest floor.

The fishing fleet exhales its fumes into the bay
Dead zones grow in concentric circles the size of trawling nets
Bringing elemental death to shore,
Hideous ruin and combustion from sea to air to land.
Yet sea otters patrol the waters below the pilings,
Foraging mussels to crack and crunch,
Twisting to drop the shells on the ocean floor.

A father exhales, breath born from fires of shame and guilt
But children in his path do not study the origins of air.
Only run. Only cower from the mighty gust that wounds
As it is formed, hurts as it hits home.
Stress cracks here appear as well,
The home has only so much hold.
Some will strengthen, some will break.

And I, standing still, exhale slowly, bracing,
Clouds escape to a frigid atmosphere warmed by carbon, blued by bullies.
All swirling, escaping, the center cannot hold.
Wroth at injustice, panicked at impending
Doom, with every slip the foundation
Edges closer to Resurrection Bay
One day to slide, suddenly swallowed.

GENERATION OF SEASONS

Spring despises summer, mocks the Fall
And flees Winter with cold dread.

Summer, proud and strong, defies all,
Its green crown trusts branch, not head.

Autumn reflects on a past soon to fall
Declines hate, gives gifts of bread.

Winter, wiser than Spring, loves all—
Drowsy and waiting, saves strength instead.

9. Intestate

. . . in which obscurity becomes the remedy,
and we join in solidarity with the dispossessed millions.

I NEVER WANT TO GO OUTSIDE

I never want to go Outside.
those hounds surround the ground
that grinds and pounds,
but here wrapped in white
and blanketed, sipping warmth
and strewn with tasty red
flowing valleys and blue hangings,
all is right.

How Ruins Get Made

The clearing stood, twinkling once,
Heading a valley; stream flowed
Out, family poured in. The homestead
Built by hands that cleared the lands
Surrounding woods and hills.

But the old Dad died inside after
The trenches of France, and later,
A tractor rolled over and killed his body,
Damaged his bride.
The farmwife followed soon after, and
The brothers began their feud.

None could live while those two fought,
And the house stood empty, windows
Broken by pebbles from wandering waifs
Let the curtains flap, the shiplap
Pulled down by needy neighbors who
Thought, "Those boys ain't using it!"

Soon the skeleton stood alone,
Sticks and stones replaced the home.
The brothers died, the feud unsolved.
The forest took the clearing back,
And just the mossy well, dry as hell, remains.

June First on the Wallace Homestead

We swung the boundary fence headed to high ridgelines
Mud, slush, rain, and shit: all standard trail hazards
On our grind up the Bald peak.
Rhythm set in with dripping red alders timing our steps,
Impromptu creek gave greeting on the path down from the heights,
But we declined its friendship.

Ahead in the aspen, a cabin crouched
Hidden, surprised, a curious inclusion on a mountainside.
It is the West, after all, the Last Frontier,
But a ghost town, just here?
We crept close, expecting prospectors or bears
To careen, but found only bullet holes and graffiti.

Seeming safe, we took in the lay: a round pond ringed
By ruined cabins, varied in decay.
Silent souls narrated every cottonwood.
A moldering stove expired near a table set for twenty.
An artesian well blasted the overfull pond,
The corral for horses that roamed the hanging valley.

Who slung hotcakes on that stove?
And whose steeds leaped those wandering creeks
Alone and on high looking down for decades
On a growing town ignorant of its watcher?

Old Til Wallace, boots caked with concrete,
Wrestled with nature and beauty and hate
And lost, turned away, abandoned the land,
Trudged down from the Eden he'd built with his hands.

WHAT WE FIND BURIED

The winter sun lay useless on the
Horizon as the chill grew confident,
And I struggled to finish shoveling.

My shovel slid like an ice skater
Abruptly stopping until the chunk
Changed the sound to deadwood.

Under the agonized poplar with
Broken arms sobbing in pain
I revealed a white bone.

Murder! My mind raced with the
Mystery as I pushed through snow
To unearth the grinning jaw.

A horse from a ghost farm had been
Planted—replete with worm-eaten
Leather saddle—in the slope.

No new horses had grown from
This crop. Snow fell like manna
As I restored the corpse to light.

My collector friend would like the
Saddle, but I eyed the skull with its
Hollow leer. The dead farmer

Had shot the beast. A perfectly
Round hole made a third eye
In the forehead. It seemed now wrong

To build a shed over a grave,
The hallowed site a monument to
Equestrian agriculture.

Shivering more with fear, I
Lifted the wizened horsehead
And the bullet fell at my feet.

Apple Core

I am standing in prison bar grass on a hill painted
Brown by summer sun
Staring up at an old man who smiles back
With apples for sale from his tree.
Me, I think, he blesses me, and I turn
Back to the house to spread manure.

Memory, my side-yard fence, snagged
My praise and cast it
Down to the spores to be gored by Loki's horns
And danced upon by cloven feet.
I questioned the blessing and the old tree,
And how my neighbors might interpret its polyphony.

Would that Plato plowed the soil next door,
He would condemn reality and the
Shadow of the tree to lie fallow
Or inspire a search for
A Real tree . . . golden limbs in a perfect
Landscape beside a cave.

My enlightened cousin, no doubt, would
Swiftly to an axe
And grind wood with blade to
Prove no man need obey one
Who seeks praise or inspiration, only firewood
And melanoma apples.

Glancing to the browning grass, I find a
Brother who would
Gather truth and beauty from her spheres;
Would tell the knighted farmer's story
And paint with brushes fine
The passion in her leaves with murder at her roots.

If it were a frosty day, another neighbor,
Younger by half,
Would harvest with an oaken ladder
In rocking sinew of pastoral youth
And speak as he did, finding wisdom in the truth,
But, perhaps, a bitterness in the fruit.

But, what of my sons? What would they see
Who perhaps someday will farmers be?
Another tree; another tree . . .
Would tree to him be twig and forest
To another?
The order of such display would suggest
Concern most technical, much delayed.

Too slow is the apple for my sons,
The poison in her seed compiles as ages done.
They would be the first to prize the sweetness
Of the flesh,
But also first to leave off eating to gasp for breath,
And the last to look for meaning,
Last to ponder reason in the artistry of God,
As fallen apples rot the moldy sod.

My sons do you tear the tree; you souls in
Dante's wood?
May you bleed as hounds grin and rape
Your horde of seeds:
A punishment most vile
To punish vile deeds.

I claimed amnesty and walked away home.
My best will broken
Toward others. My friends asleep
And silent to my calls,
My brothers dead and buried in their vaults,
While my children rolled out biscuits for the morn
Greased with lard and bacon with which to fill their hoard,
My apples stayed with me. And I remained forlorn.

This is How I Go

Let us descend now into this deep menu—
Hollows ring with possibility—
Stubborn tumor or avalanche?
Spinal virus or seeping neutrons?

Lest we play victim and weep premature
At the hundreds of options
Whose details obscure which plague
Will descend and whose roots will endure,
Remember one fact, one truth secure:
This is how I go.

But bitter is the veil, hidden antecedent
The only fear to feel
If only he would reveal, all others
Could fade into I don't care.
In twenty years or more, when
I've crept closer to that dark door
Perhaps then figures carved will sharpen,
Clarify, and resolve into adieux.
There I may scry the script at its core:
This is how I go.

But trivial now are such fears.
With certainty, only one may reign,
And when it appears
My eyes will close
My breath subside
Yet fear is the demon whose
Grip must give.
Why fear sleep? Why flee from soldiers
Who must surely conquer?
Why quest to know what cannot be known
To sacrifice life on an altar of groans?

Maybe this is how I go,
But until then leap, not merely tiptoe.

Obscurity

Take no notice,
Wrap me instead in valleys
Perfumed with salmon-scented rowan.
Shroud my footfalls with rain-soaked sphagnum
To muffle my passing.

Hide me beneath the canopy
And pass by.
What highs or lows need break through the birdsong?
Warblers shout down headlines,
As swallows snatch their peaceful meals over fields.

Keep your noisy fame,
Your notice and your self-awareness.
Mine are the shadows, the distant deeps,
And the unsung acts praised only by memory.
Then bury me, unmarked and ignored, a contented pauper
By none adored.